ISHWAR CHANDRA
VIDYASAGAR

LEGENDS AND LEGACIES

THE BIOGRAPHY OF
ISHWAR CHANDRA VIDYASAGAR

RUPA

Published by
Rupa Publications India Pvt. Ltd 2024
7/16, Ansari Road, Daryaganj
New Delhi 110002

Sales centres:
Bengaluru Chennai
Hyderabad Jaipur Kathmandu
Kolkata Mumbai Prayagraj

Copyright © Rupa Publications India Pvt. Ltd 2024

The views and opinions expressed in this book are the author's own and the facts are as reported by him which have been verified to the extent possible, and the publishers are not in any way liable for the same.

All rights reserved.
No part of this publication may be reproduced, transmitted, or stored in a retrieval system, in any form or by any means, electronic, mechanical, photocopying, recording or otherwise, without the prior permission of the publisher.

P-ISBN: 978-93-6156-512-0
E-ISBN: 978-93-6156-721-6

First impression 2024

10 9 8 7 6 5 4 3 2 1

Printed in India

This book is sold subject to the condition that it shall not, by way of trade or otherwise, be lent, resold, hired out, or otherwise circulated, without the publisher's prior consent, in any form of binding or cover other than that in which it is published.

Contents

Introduction	7
Early Life (1820 to 1828)	9
Education (1829-1841)	14
Teaching and Career (1841-1850)	21
Social Reforms (1850-1860)	29
Language and Literature (1851-1870)	36
Published Works of Ishwar Chandra Vidyasagar	45
Personal Life (1820-1891)	48
Legacy (1891-Present)	57
His Interests	63
Conclusion	74
Timeline of Ishwar Chandra Vidyasagar's Life	76
Excerpts from Vidyasagar's Works	78

Introduction

Ishwar Chandra Vidyasagar was a remarkable scholar, educator, and social reformer from India. Born on September 26, 1820, in the small village of Birsingha in Bengal, he rose from humble beginnings to become one of the most respected and influential figures in Indian history. His full name was Ishwar Chandra Bandopadhyay, but he earned the title "Vidyasagar," meaning "Ocean of Knowledge," because of his vast learning and scholarship.

Ishwar Chandra Vidyasagar

From a young age, Vidyasagar showed an extraordinary love for learning. Despite his family's poverty, which made life difficult, he excelled in his studies through sheer determination and hard work. His dedication earned him many scholarships, allowing him to continue his education at the prestigious Sanskrit College in Kolkata. There, he became a brilliant student of Sanskrit and other subjects, quickly gaining a reputation for his intellectual abilities.

But Vidyasagar was more than just a scholar; he was a compassionate individual deeply concerned with the welfare of others. He believed that knowledge should be used to improve society and make life better for everyone, particularly those who were less fortunate. This belief motivated him to work tirelessly for educational reforms, women's rights, and social change throughout his life.

Ishwar Chandra Vidyasagar's importance lies in his significant contributions to education, social reform, and literature in India. He is remembered and respected for several key reasons.

First and foremost, Vidyasagar was a pioneer in educational reform. He believed that education was the cornerstone of a better society and worked diligently to make it accessible to everyone, including girls and people from disadvantaged backgrounds. He played a crucial role in modernizing the education system in Bengal, introducing Western ideas and subjects alongside traditional Indian teachings. His efforts included writing many textbooks that were used in schools for many years, helping to shape the minds of countless young students.

In addition to his work in education, Vidyasagar was a strong advocate for women's rights at a time when women in India faced numerous hardships and injustices. He campaigned vigorously for the right of widows to remarry, a practice that was largely forbidden and stigmatized in his society. His relentless efforts led to the passage of the Widow Remarriage Act in 1856, which was a monumental step towards improving the lives of countless women. Vidyasagar also worked to promote women's education, believing that educated women could contribute significantly to the progress of society.

Vidyasagar simplified the Bengali alphabet and grammar, making the language easier to learn and use. This not only helped to increase literacy rates but also enriched Bengali literature, allowing more people to access and appreciate literary works. His own writings, which include textbooks and literary works, continue to be celebrated for their clarity and insight.

Beyond his specific achievements, Vidyasagar's legacy endures because of his unwavering commitment to social justice and human dignity. He demonstrated that one person, driven by knowledge and compassion, could bring about meaningful change in society. His life and work remain an inspiration, encouraging us to strive for a world where education is accessible to all, and where everyone is treated with respect and fairness.

1
Early Life (1820 to 1828)

Ishwar Chandra Vidyasagar, a revered figure in Indian history, was born on September 26, 1820, in a small village called Birsingha in the Midnapore district of Bengal, India. His birth name was Ishwar Chandra Bandopadhyay. The family later adopted the name Vidyasagar, meaning "Ocean of Knowledge," which was a testament to his incredible intellect and contributions to education and society.

House of Vidyasagar at Vidysagar Street, Kolkata

Ishwar Chandra was born into a poor but respectable Brahmin family. His father, Thakurdas Bandyopadhyay, was a modest man who worked as a temple priest and struggled to make ends meet. His mother, Bhagavati Devi, was a deeply religious and kind-hearted woman who had a significant influence on young Ishwar's upbringing. Despite their limited financial resources, Thakurdas and Bhagavati were determined to provide their children with a good education, valuing learning and moral integrity above all else.

Childhood Adventures

Growing up in the rural setting of Birsingha, Ishwar Chandra experienced a childhood filled with simplicity and nature. The lush green fields, the songs of birds, and the tranquil environment of the village formed the backdrop of his early years. However, life was not without its hardships. The family's financial struggles meant that luxuries were out of reach, and even basic necessities were hard to come by at times.

Despite these challenges, Ishwar Chandra's childhood was marked by curiosity and a thirst for knowledge. He was a bright and inquisitive child, always eager to learn and explore. His mother played a crucial role in fostering this love for learning. She often told him stories from the Ramayana and Mahabharata, which not only entertained him but also instilled in him the values of courage, righteousness, and compassion.

One of the popular anecdotes from his childhood highlights his insatiable curiosity. It is said that Ishwar Chandra was once so captivated by the sight of a street lamp that he stayed up all night reading under its light because there was no lamp at home. This determination and love for reading became a hallmark of his character.

Early Education at Home

Ishwar Chandra's early education began at home under the guidance of his mother and later his father. Bhagavati Devi, although not formally educated, was well-versed in religious texts and the Bengali language. She taught him the Bengali alphabet and basic arithmetic, laying a strong foundation for his future education. Her patient and loving approach to teaching made learning enjoyable for Ishwar Chandra.

Bhagavati Devi,
mother of Vidyasagar

Thakurdas Bandyopadhyay,
father of Vidyasagar

Thakurdas Bandyopadhyay, despite his busy schedule as a priest, took time to teach his son Sanskrit. Recognizing Ishwar Chandra's exceptional intellect, he introduced him to various religious scriptures and classical literature. Thakurdas was a strict disciplinarian and insisted on rigorous study routines. Ishwar Chandra's early exposure to these texts not only honed his linguistic skills but also instilled in him a deep appreciation for his cultural heritage.

At a very young age, Ishwar Chandra displayed a remarkable ability to memorize complex verses and understand difficult concepts. His prodigious memory and comprehension skills amazed everyone around him. His family, recognizing his potential, encouraged him to pursue higher education, despite the financial challenges they faced.

Love for Learning

Ishwar Chandra Vidyasagar's love for learning was evident from his early years. His passion for knowledge transcended the limited resources available to him. He was not content with just the basics; he yearned to learn more and delve deeper into various subjects.

One significant factor that fueled his love for learning was his exposure to the vibrant intellectual culture of Bengal during the early 19th century. This was a period of social and intellectual awakening in Bengal, often referred to as the Bengal Renaissance. Influential thinkers, writers, and reformers like Raja Ram Mohan Roy were advocating for education, social reforms, and a revival of Indian culture. Ishwar Chandra was greatly inspired by these movements and aspired to contribute to the intellectual and social advancement of his community.

To pursue his education, Ishwar Chandra had to overcome numerous obstacles. The nearest school was in the town of Calcutta (now Kolkata), which was a considerable distance from his village. However, his determination knew no bounds. At the age of nine, he set out on foot with his father to Calcutta, braving long and arduous journeys, to seek admission to a school that could provide him with a more formal education.

In Calcutta, Ishwar Chandra enrolled in a local school where he continued to excel. His teachers were impressed by his dedication and brilliance. He quickly mastered subjects like Sanskrit, Bengali, and English. His passion for learning was not limited to the classroom; he spent countless hours in libraries, reading everything he could get his hands on.

Despite the financial strain on his family, Ishwar Chandra never lost sight of his goal. He took on various part-time jobs to support himself and his education. From tutoring younger students to working as a scribe, he did whatever it took to continue his studies. His perseverance and hard work paid off when he won several scholarships, which eased the financial burden on his family.

His deep love for learning and his commitment to education eventually led him to Sanskrit College in Calcutta, one of the premier institutions of higher learning at the time. Here, he further honed his skills and gained profound knowledge in subjects like Sanskrit grammar, literature, and philosophy. His academic excellence earned him the title of "Vidyasagar," which means "Ocean of Knowledge," a name that perfectly encapsulated his vast intellect and scholarly achievements.

Ishwar Chandra Vidyasagar's early life laid the foundation for his future accomplishments. Born into a humble family in a small village, he faced numerous challenges, but his indomitable spirit and unwavering love for learning propelled him forward. His childhood adventures, early education at home, and relentless pursuit of knowledge not only shaped his character but also set the stage for his remarkable contributions to Indian society and education.

His story is a testament to the power of determination and the transformative impact of education. Despite the odds, Ishwar Chandra Vidyasagar emerged as one of the greatest scholars and social reformers of his time, leaving an indelible mark on history. His early years serve as an inspiration for children and adults alike, reminding us that with passion, hard work, and a thirst for knowledge, we can overcome any obstacle and achieve greatness.

2

Education (1829-1841)

Early Education and Exceptional Memory

Ishwar Chandra Vidyasagar's educational journey is a testament to his remarkable intellect and insatiable thirst for knowledge. From a young age, he exhibited an extraordinary memory, a gift that set him apart from his peers. He could recite entire books and scriptures from memory, impressing both his teachers and fellow students. This ability was not just a natural talent but also a result of his disciplined study habits and relentless dedication to learning.

Despite his growing fame as a scholar, Vidyasagar remained modest and humble throughout his life. He shunned the trappings of luxury, choosing instead to lead a simple lifestyle. His focus was always on his studies and the betterment of society rather than personal gain or recognition. This humility endeared him to many and made his scholarly achievements even more admirable.

School Days in Calcutta (1829)

In 1829, at the tender age of nine, Ishwar Chandra Vidyasagar, accompanied by his father Thakurdas Bandyopadhyay, embarked on a significant journey from their village, Birsingha, to the bustling city of Calcutta (now Kolkata). This move was driven by the desire to provide young Ishwar with better educational opportunities, as

Calcutta was known for its schools and intellectual environment.

Upon reaching Calcutta, Ishwar Chandra was enrolled in the local primary school, a modest institution where his academic journey took a more formal shape. The transition from the serene village life to the vibrant and chaotic city was challenging, but Ishwar Chandra's excitement to learn overshadowed any discomfort. The city, with its libraries, books, and diverse intellectual activities, became a playground for his curious mind.

In school, Ishwar Chandra quickly distinguished himself as an exceptional student. His proficiency in Bengali, Sanskrit, and mathematics amazed his teachers. Despite the limited resources, his thirst for knowledge drove him to spend hours reading and studying, often under the dim light of street lamps due to the lack of proper lighting at home.

> **Fun Fact**
> During his time in Calcutta, Vidyasagar was known to walk long distances, often barefoot, to attend classes and access libraries, showcasing his immense dedication to learning.

Overcoming Obstacles

While Calcutta offered better educational resources, it also presented numerous challenges. The primary obstacle was financial. Ishwar Chandra's family was not affluent, and supporting his education in the city was a significant strain on their meager resources. Thakurdas, who had accompanied his son, struggled to find consistent work, adding to their financial difficulties.

To mitigate this, Ishwar Chandra took on various part-time jobs. He tutored younger students, worked as a scribe, and did any work that came his way, all while continuing his studies. His resilience and dedication were remarkable; he never let these hardships deter him from his educational goals.

Another major challenge was the cultural adjustment. Coming from a rural village, Ishwar Chandra had to adapt to the urban environment of Calcutta, which was a melting pot of different cultures and ideas. This required not just academic adjustment but also social and emotional resilience. However, Ishwar Chandra's adaptability and open-mindedness helped him overcome these barriers, and he soon thrived in the city's diverse intellectual atmosphere.

Studying at Sanskrit College (1829-1841)

Sanskrit College, Calcutta

Ishwar Chandra Vidyasagar's academic brilliance did not go unnoticed. In 1829, the same year he arrived in Calcutta, he was admitted to the prestigious Sanskrit College. Established in 1824, Sanskrit College was one of the foremost institutions of higher learning in India, focusing on the study of Sanskrit literature, grammar, and philosophy. This institution played a crucial role in shaping Vidyasagar's intellectual and ideological foundations.

At Sanskrit College, Ishwar Chandra's intellect truly blossomed. He delved deeply into the study of Sanskrit grammar, literature, and classical texts. His ability to grasp complex concepts quickly earned him the respect of his peers and teachers. The rigorous curriculum, which included subjects like Vedic studies, Vedanta philosophy, and Nyaya (logic), was challenging, but Ishwar Chandra thrived in this environment.

> **Fun Fact**
> Vidyasagar's ability to recite large portions of the text from memory astonished his peers and even senior scholars.

One of his most notable achievements at Sanskrit College was his mastery of the "Siddhanta Kaumudi," a comprehensive treatise on Sanskrit grammar. It is said that he memorized the entire text, a feat that earned him the admiration of his professors and the title "Vidyasagar" (Ocean of Knowledge). His knowledge was not just theoretical; he could apply complex grammatical rules practically, showcasing his deep understanding of the subject.

Beyond his academic pursuits, Vidyasagar was known for his extraordinary work ethic and dedication to his studies. He would often wake up before dawn to study by the dim light of oil lamps, a testament to his determination and love for learning. His disciplined routine included hours of reading, writing, and engaging in intellectual discussions, setting a high standard for his fellow students.

During his time at Sanskrit College, Ishwar Chandra also developed a keen interest in the social issues of his time. He was influenced by the intellectual and reformist currents flowing through Bengal, particularly the works of Raja Ram Mohan Roy. This exposure sowed the seeds for his future role as a social reformer. Vidyasagar's engagement with these ideas led him to question traditional practices and advocate for progressive changes in society.

A lesser-known aspect of Vidyasagar's college life was his involvement in extracurricular activities. He was an avid participant in debates and literary clubs, where he honed his oratory skills and developed a keen sense of rhetoric and argumentation. These activities not only enhanced his intellectual capabilities but also prepared him for his future role as a reformer and educator.

Vidyasagar's time at Sanskrit College was also marked by his interactions with a diverse group of students and scholars. These interactions broadened his perspective and deepened his understanding of different cultural and philosophical viewpoints. His ability to engage with and appreciate diverse opinions made him a respected figure among his peers.

During his college years, Vidyasagar also faced personal and financial hardships. Despite these challenges, he remained focused on his studies and never allowed adversity to deter him from his goals. His resilience and perseverance became sources of inspiration for his contemporaries and future generations.

In addition to his academic and social pursuits, Vidyasagar was known for his sense of humor and storytelling abilities. He often used anecdotes and humorous tales to illustrate complex points during lectures, making his classes both informative and engaging. His wit and eloquence made him a beloved figure among students and teachers alike.

Ishwar Chandra Vidyasagar's years at Sanskrit College were transformative, laying the foundation for his future endeavors as a scholar, educator, and social reformer. His intellectual growth, coupled with his commitment to social justice, set the stage for his later contributions to Indian society. His legacy as a student at Sanskrit College continues to inspire and guide those who seek knowledge and aspire to make a positive impact on the world.

Becoming a Scholar (1841)

By 1841, after twelve years of rigorous study, Ishwar Chandra Vidyasagar had transformed from a curious village boy into a distinguished scholar. His academic excellence was recognized with the highest honors from Sanskrit College, cementing his reputation as one of the brightest minds of his generation. In the same year, he was appointed as the head pandit (scholar) of the Fort William College, a significant position that marked the beginning of his professional career. Fort William College was an institution established by the British East India Company to train their officers in Indian languages and culture. In this role, Ishwar Chandra was responsible for teaching and translating texts, which further honed his linguistic skills and deepened his understanding of both Indian and Western knowledge systems.

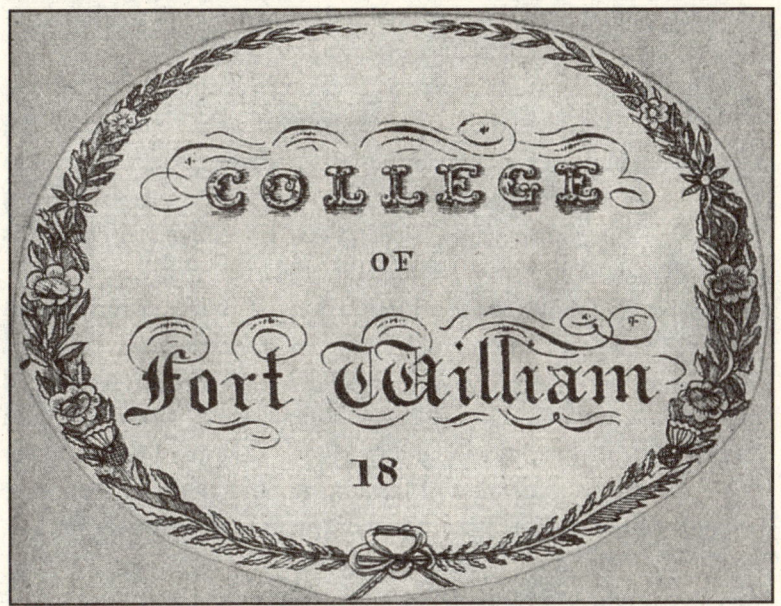

Fort William College, Library Board

His scholarly achievements went beyond mere academic recognition. Ishwar Chandra's work began to have a practical impact on society. His efforts to simplify and modernize the Bengali language made it more accessible to the common people, fostering a greater spread of literacy and education. He believed that

Fun Fact

Vidyasagar personally oversaw the illustrations in "Bodhodaya," understanding that visual aids could significantly enhance a child's learning experience. He collaborated with local artists to ensure that the images were both educational and culturally relevant.

education was the key to social reform and dedicated his life to making it available to all, regardless of caste or gender.

Moreover, his time at Fort William College exposed him to Western ideas and philosophies, which he critically analyzed and incorporated into his vision for a reformed Indian society. He understood the importance of combining the best elements of both Indian and Western educational systems, which later influenced his educational reforms.

The period from 1829 to 1841 was transformative for Ishwar Chandra Vidyasagar. His journey from a small village to the intellectual hubs of Calcutta and Sanskrit College shaped him into a scholar of unparalleled depth and insight. Despite numerous obstacles, his unwavering dedication to education and his insatiable curiosity propelled him forward.

These years laid the foundation for his future contributions as an educator, reformer, and writer. His academic achievements, coupled with his deep sense of social responsibility, positioned him as a leading figure in the Bengal Renaissance. Ishwar Chandra Vidyasagar's early educational journey is a testament to the power of perseverance, the value of hard work, and the transformative impact of education. His life story continues to inspire generations, reminding us that with determination and a passion for learning, we can overcome any challenge and achieve greatness.

3

Teaching and Career (1841-1850)

First Job as a Teacher (1841)

In 1841, at the age of 21, Ishwar Chandra Vidyasagar began his professional career as a teacher. His first job was as the head pandit (scholar) of Fort William College in Calcutta. This institution, established by the British East India Company, aimed to train their officers in Indian languages and culture. Vidyasagar's role at the college involved teaching Sanskrit and Bengali to British officials, as well as translating important texts.

Ex-libris from the Fort William College Library

At Fort William College, Vidyasagar quickly distinguished himself through his profound knowledge and effective teaching methods. His ability to simplify complex grammatical and literary concepts made him an invaluable asset to the institution. He worked diligently to bridge the cultural and linguistic gaps between the British officers and the Indian populace, ensuring that the officers could communicate effectively and understand Indian traditions and customs.

During this period, Vidyasagar also interacted with various scholars and intellectuals, both Indian and British, which broadened his perspectives and enriched his understanding of different educational philosophies. These interactions played a crucial role in shaping his own views on education and reform.

Teaching Philosophy

Ishwar Chandra Vidyasagar's teaching philosophy was deeply influenced by his own educational experiences and the intellectual environment of the time. He believed that education should be accessible to all, regardless of caste, gender, or social status. This egalitarian view was revolutionary in a society where education was often restricted to the upper castes and men.

Vidyasagar's teaching philosophy can be summarized through several key principles:

1. *Accessibility and Inclusivity:* Vidyasagar advocated for the democratization of education. He believed that everyone, including women and lower-caste individuals, had the right to education. This belief was reflected in his efforts to establish schools that were open to all.
2. *Practical and Relevant Curriculum:* He emphasized the importance of a practical and relevant curriculum that could equip students with the skills needed for everyday life. Vidyasagar argued that education should not only focus on

classical languages and literature but also include subjects like mathematics, science, and modern languages.

3. ***Moral and Ethical Education:*** Vidyasagar believed that education should not just impart knowledge but also inculcate moral and ethical values. He often integrated lessons on honesty, integrity, and social responsibility into his teaching.

4. ***Simplification of Language:*** Recognizing the barriers posed by the complexity of Sanskrit and classical Bengali, Vidyasagar worked to simplify the Bengali language, making it more accessible to the common people. He wrote textbooks that were easy to understand, ensuring that students from all backgrounds could benefit from them.

5. ***Encouragement of Critical Thinking:*** Vidyasagar encouraged his students to think critically and question established norms. He believed that education should foster independent thinking and problem-solving abilities rather than rote memorization.

> **Fun Fact**
>
> While translating "Rajatarangini," Vidyasagar made extensive notes and commentaries to explain historical contexts and references, providing readers with a deeper understanding of the text. These notes are valuable resources for scholars studying the period.

Contributions to Education

Ishwar Chandra Vidyasagar's contributions to education were profound and multifaceted. His efforts significantly transformed the educational landscape of Bengal and had a lasting impact on Indian society. Some of his major contributions include:

1. ***Modernization of Bengali Language and Literature:*** One of Vidyasagar's most notable contributions was the simplification and modernization of the Bengali language. He introduced punctuation marks in Bengali prose and standardized the language, making it more coherent and accessible. His textbooks

on Bengali grammar and literature became foundational texts for students and scholars alike.
2. **Development of Educational Textbooks:** Understanding the need for quality educational materials, Vidyasagar wrote and compiled several textbooks on various subjects, including grammar, literature, and arithmetic. His books, such as "Bodhodaya" (Dawn of Knowledge), were widely used in schools and played a crucial role in improving literacy rates.
3. **Establishment of Schools:** Vidyasagar was instrumental in establishing numerous schools across Bengal, particularly for girls. He founded several schools that provided education to children from different socio-economic backgrounds. His efforts to promote women's education were pioneering and laid the groundwork for future advancements in this area.
4. **Promotion of Women's Education:** Vidyasagar was a staunch advocate for women's education, a radical idea in 19th-century India. He believed that educating women was essential for the progress of society. To this end, he established several schools for girls and worked tirelessly to convince families to send their daughters to school. His efforts faced significant resistance, but his perseverance eventually led to increased acceptance of women's education.
5. **Educational Reforms:** As an educationist, Vidyasagar introduced several reforms aimed at improving the quality and accessibility of education. He advocated for the inclusion of vernacular languages in the curriculum, the adoption of modern teaching methods, and the establishment of training institutes for teachers.
6. **Role in Founding the Calcutta University:** Vidyasagar played a key role in the establishment of Calcutta University in 1857. He was a member of the committee that worked on the formation of the university, which aimed to provide higher education and promote research in various fields.

Principal of Sanskrit College (1851)

In 1851, Ishwar Chandra Vidyasagar was appointed as the principal of Sanskrit College in Calcutta, a prestigious institution dedicated to the study of Sanskrit and classical Indian literature. His appointment marked a significant milestone in his career and provided him with a platform to implement his educational ideals on a larger scale.

As the principal, Vidyasagar initiated several reforms to modernize the college and make it more inclusive:

1. **Curriculum Reforms:** Vidyasagar expanded the curriculum to include subjects such as English, mathematics, and science, alongside traditional Sanskrit studies. He believed that a comprehensive education should encompass both classical and modern knowledge.
2. **Promotion of English Education:** While deeply rooted in Indian traditions, Vidyasagar recognized the importance of English education in the context of British India. He introduced English as a subject at Sanskrit College, ensuring that students could gain proficiency in the language and access a wider range of knowledge and opportunities.
3. **Scholarship Programs:** Understanding the financial constraints faced by many students, Vidyasagar established scholarship programs to support deserving students from economically disadvantaged backgrounds. These scholarships enabled many talented individuals to pursue their education without financial burden.
4. **Teacher Training:** Vidyasagar emphasized the importance of well-trained teachers in delivering quality education. He organized training programs for the college's faculty, encouraging them to adopt modern teaching methods and stay updated with the latest developments in their respective fields.
5. **Infrastructure Development:** Under his leadership, Sanskrit College saw significant improvements in its infrastructure. Vidyasagar worked to enhance the library, classrooms, and

other facilities, creating a conducive environment for learning and research.

Other Important Positions

In addition to his role at Sanskrit College, Ishwar Chandra Vidyasagar held several other important positions that allowed him to influence education and social reform across Bengal:

1. **Secretary of the Sanskrit College:** As the secretary, Vidyasagar played a crucial role in the administration and governance of the college. He used this position to advocate for further reforms and improvements in the institution.
2. **Inspector of Schools:** Vidyasagar was appointed as the special inspector of schools for the southern districts of Bengal. In this capacity, he traveled extensively to inspect schools, assess their performance, and implement necessary reforms. His efforts led to the establishment of more schools and an improvement in the quality of education in these districts.
3. **Member of the Education Commission:** Vidyasagar served as a member of the Education Commission, where he worked alongside other eminent educators and reformers to formulate policies aimed at improving the educational system in Bengal. His insights and recommendations were instrumental in shaping the commission's policies.
4. **Social Reformer and Writer:** Alongside his educational endeavors, Vidyasagar continued to be an active social reformer and writer. He wrote extensively on social issues, advocating for widow remarriage, the abolition of child marriage, and the upliftment of women and lower-caste individuals. His writings had a profound impact on public opinion and helped pave the way for legislative reforms.

The period from 1841 to 1850 was a defining phase in Ishwar Chandra Vidyasagar's life, marked by his contributions as a teacher, administrator, and reformer. His first job as a teacher at Fort William College set the stage for his illustrious career, where

Pundit Ishwar Chandra Vidyasagar

he distinguished himself through his profound knowledge and effective teaching methods.

Vidyasagar's teaching philosophy, centered on accessibility, practical relevance, moral education, language simplification, and critical thinking, was revolutionary for his time. His contributions to education, including the modernization of the Bengali language, development of educational textbooks, establishment of schools, promotion of women's education, and educational reforms, had a lasting impact on Indian society.

As the principal of Sanskrit College, Vidyasagar implemented significant reforms that modernized the institution and made it more inclusive. His leadership and vision transformed the college into a center of excellence, blending traditional and modern knowledge.

Beyond Sanskrit College, Vidyasagar held various important positions that allowed him to influence education and social reform across Bengal. His efforts as a secretary, inspector of schools, and member of the Education Commission, along with his work as a social reformer and writer, cemented his legacy as one of the greatest educators and reformers in Indian history.

Ishwar Chandra Vidyasagar's life and work continue to inspire generations, reminding us of the transformative power of education and the importance of perseverance, dedication, and a commitment to social justice. His contributions laid the foundation for a more inclusive and progressive society, and his legacy lives on in the educational and social advancements that followed.

4

Social Reforms (1850-1860)

The Plight of Widows

During the mid-19th century in India, the plight of widows was a stark reflection of the deep-seated social inequalities and oppressive customs prevalent in society. Widows, especially those from higher castes, faced severe ostracism and deprivation following the death of their husbands. The prevalent customs mandated that widows shave their heads, discard all colored clothing for stark white garments, and lead lives of austerity and seclusion. This practice, reinforced by societal norms and religious dogma, subjected widows to profound social stigma and denied them basic human dignity.

For Ishwar Chandra Vidyasagar, witnessing the suffering of widows was a deeply unsettling experience. Raised in an environment influenced by progressive ideas of the Bengal Renaissance, Vidyasagar was acutely aware of the moral and humanitarian imperatives to challenge these oppressive practices. His advocacy for social reform was rooted in a profound

> **Fun Fact**
> Vidyasagar's "Sitar Banabas" was a subtle yet powerful commentary on the status of women in society. Through this work, he highlighted the injustices faced by women and advocated for their rights and dignity. This book reflected his deep commitment to social reform and gender equality.

sense of empathy and a firm belief in the principles of justice and equality.

Campaign for Widow Remarriage (1855)

In 1855, Ishwar Chandra Vidyasagar launched a courageous campaign to advocate for the remarriage of Hindu widows. Central to his campaign was the conviction that denying widows the right to remarry was not only unjust but also contrary to the true spirit of Hinduism. Vidyasagar meticulously researched ancient Hindu scriptures and texts, arguing that many revered texts did not prohibit widow remarriage. He contended that such prohibitions were later additions that contradicted the inclusive and humane essence of Hindu philosophy.

Armed with his scholarly insights and unwavering determination, Vidyasagar penned persuasive articles in both Bengali and English, disseminating his arguments to a wide audience. He actively engaged with community leaders, intellectuals, and reformers, urging them to join his cause. His campaign quickly gained momentum, sparking intense debates and discussions across Bengal.

Opposition and Success

Despite Vidyasagar's compelling arguments and moral clarity, his campaign encountered fierce opposition from entrenched conservative forces within Indian society. Orthodox religious leaders, traditionalists, and those vested in maintaining the status quo vehemently opposed his efforts. They viewed widow remarriage as a threat to established social hierarchies and religious norms, fearing that it would destabilize traditional family structures.

Vidyasagar faced personal attacks and slander from his critics, who accused him of blasphemy and attempting to subvert Hindu traditions. However, he remained steadfast in his convictions, undeterred by the backlash. His courage and persistence in the face of adversity underscored his commitment to justice and reform.

The turning point in Vidyasagar's campaign came with the passage of the Hindu Widows' Remarriage Act in 1856 by the British government. This landmark legislation legalized widow remarriage and represented a significant triumph for Vidyasagar and the broader social reform movement in India. The passage of the Act was a testament to Vidyasagar's strategic advocacy and the growing support for progressive reforms.

Work for Women's Education

Beyond his advocacy for widow remarriage, Ishwar Chandra Vidyasagar was a pioneering advocate for women's education in India. Recognizing that education was the cornerstone of empowerment, Vidyasagar believed fervently in the transformative potential of education for women. He understood that educating women was not merely about imparting knowledge but also about fostering independence, critical thinking, and social awareness.

In 1849, Vidyasagar established the first girls' school in Calcutta, breaking new ground in a society where female education was often neglected or actively discouraged. The school provided girls with a comprehensive education that included subjects such as Bengali, Sanskrit, mathematics, and moral sciences. Vidyasagar ensured that the curriculum was designed to nurture well-rounded individuals capable of contributing meaningfully to society.

The establishment of girls' schools was not without its challenges. Vidyasagar faced staunch opposition from conservative elements who viewed female education as a threat to traditional gender roles and societal norms. Families were hesitant to send their daughters to school due to fears of social stigma and concerns about the impact on marriage prospects.

Undeterred by these obstacles, Vidyasagar personally visited families, advocating passionately for the benefits of education for girls. He appealed to parents' sense of responsibility and enlightened self-interest, persuading them that educated daughters would be better equipped to navigate a changing world and contribute positively to their families and communities.

Vidyasagar's efforts to promote women's education extended beyond Calcutta. He established several schools for girls across Bengal, ensuring that education was accessible to girls from diverse socio-economic backgrounds. His visionary leadership laid the foundation for significant advancements in women's education in India, inspiring future generations of educators and reformers to prioritize gender equality and social justice.

Other Social Initiatives

In addition to his pivotal roles in advocating for widow remarriage and promoting women's education, Ishwar Chandra Vidyasagar was actively involved in a range of other social initiatives aimed at improving the welfare of marginalized communities and fostering social reform in India.

Abolition of Polygamy: Vidyasagar vehemently opposed the practice of polygamy, which was prevalent among certain sections of Bengali society. He argued that polygamy perpetuated gender inequality and exploitation, particularly of women. His advocacy contributed to a growing awareness of the need to reform marriage practices and uphold principles of equality and justice.

Promotion of Vernacular Education: Recognizing the importance of language in education, Vidyasagar was a passionate advocate for vernacular education. He believed that education in one's mother tongue was essential for effective learning and encouraged the development and standardization of the Bengali language. His efforts to promote vernacular education played a crucial role in expanding access to education among the Bengali-speaking population.

Advocacy for Legal Reforms: Vidyasagar actively engaged with British officials and Indian reformers to advocate for legal reforms aimed at addressing social injustices and advancing progressive causes. His contributions to legal reforms were instrumental in shaping legislation that sought to protect the rights of marginalized communities, including women and lower-caste individuals.

Public Health and Sanitation: Vidyasagar recognized the importance of public health and sanitation in improving the quality of life for all members of society. He campaigned for better sanitary conditions in Calcutta and raised awareness about the importance of hygiene and cleanliness. His efforts contributed to improvements in public health standards and set a precedent for future initiatives in public health.

Philanthropy: Known for his compassion and generosity, Vidyasagar dedicated a significant portion of his earnings to philanthropic causes. He supported educational institutions, orphanages, and charitable organizations that provided assistance to the needy and marginalized. His philanthropic efforts reflected his commitment to social welfare and his belief in the importance of giving back to the community.

Legacy and Impact

Ishwar Chandra Vidyasagar's legacy continues to resonate deeply in India and beyond, enduring as a testament to his unwavering commitment to social justice, equality, and human dignity. His pioneering efforts in advocating for widow remarriage and promoting women's education challenged entrenched social norms and laid the foundation for significant social reforms in Indian society.

Empowerment of Women: Vidyasagar's advocacy for widow remarriage and women's education played a pivotal role in empowering women and expanding their opportunities for personal and intellectual growth. By challenging discriminatory practices and advocating for women's rights, he helped to dismantle barriers that had long restricted women's autonomy and participation in society.

Educational Reforms: Vidyasagar's contributions to education were transformative, particularly his efforts to promote vernacular education and expand access to quality schooling. His establishment of girls' schools and advocacy for inclusive educational practices set a precedent for future reforms aimed at democratizing education and empowering marginalized communities.

Social Justice and Equality: Throughout his career, Vidyasagar remained steadfast in his commitment to social justice and equality. His advocacy for legal reforms and his efforts to challenge caste-based discrimination and gender inequality laid the groundwork for a more inclusive and equitable society. His legacy continues to inspire ongoing efforts to address social injustices and uphold human rights.

Philanthropy and Compassion: Vidyasagar's philanthropic endeavors exemplified his compassion for the less fortunate and his belief in the importance of collective responsibility. His generous contributions to charitable causes helped to alleviate suffering and improve the welfare of marginalized communities. His legacy serves as a reminder of the enduring impact of compassion and generosity in creating positive social change.

Inspiration for Future Reformers: Ishwar Chandra Vidyasagar's life and work continue to inspire generations of reformers, educators, and activists who are committed to advancing social justice and human rights. His example demonstrates the transformative power of courage, compassion, and dedication in confronting injustice and striving for a more just and equitable society.

Ishwar Chandra Vidyasagar's contributions to social reform during the period from 1850 to 1860 epitomize the spirit of resilience, compassion, and unwavering commitment to justice. His advocacy for widow remarriage, promotion of women's education, and broader social initiatives challenged the status quo and laid the foundation for a more equitable society. His legacy as a visionary thinker, educator, and social reformer continues to resonate today, serving as a beacon of hope and inspiration for all those who strive to create a world where dignity, equality, and compassion prevail.

By courageously confronting social injustices and advocating for transformative change, Vidyasagar exemplified the transformative power of individual action and collective effort in advancing human rights and social progress. His life and work remind us of the enduring importance of compassion, empathy, and solidarity in building a society where every individual can flourish and contribute meaningfully to the common good.

In honoring Ishwar Chandra Vidyasagar's legacy, we reaffirm our commitment to upholding the values of justice, equality, and human dignity. His pioneering efforts continue to guide us on the path towards a more inclusive and just world, inspiring future generations to embrace the mantle of leadership in advancing social reform and building a brighter future for all.

As we reflect on Vidyasagar's enduring legacy, we are reminded of his timeless message: that each of us has the power to make a difference, to challenge injustice, and to champion the rights of the marginalized. In doing so, we honor not only his memory but also the principles for which he tirelessly fought throughout his life.

5
Language and Literature (1851-1870)

Simplifying Bengali

Ishwar Chandra Vidyasagar's work in simplifying the Bengali language was pivotal in making it accessible to the common people. During the mid-19th century, Bengali was heavily influenced by Sanskrit, which made it complex and difficult for the average person to understand. This complexity was a significant barrier to education and literacy, particularly among the lower classes and children. Vidyasagar, with his vision of an enlightened and educated society, embarked on a mission to transform the Bengali language.

1. **Simplified Grammar:** Vidyasagar recognized that the intricate grammar rules derived from Sanskrit were a major obstacle. He revised the grammatical structure of Bengali to make it simpler and more user-friendly. This included the simplification of verb conjugations, sentence constructions, and the reduction of complex syntactic forms. His work made the language more intuitive and easier to learn, especially for beginners.
2. **Reduction of Sanskrit Influence:** The heavy reliance on Sanskrit vocabulary in Bengali made the language seem elite and distant from everyday life. Vidyasagar systematically reduced the use of Sanskrit words, replacing them with simpler, colloquial alternatives. This effort was aimed at demystifying the language and making it more relatable and usable by the mass-

es. By doing so, he bridged the gap between the written and spoken forms of Bengali, making written texts more accessible.
3. **Standardization:** One of Vidyasagar's significant contributions was the standardization of Bengali spelling and grammar. Before his reforms, there were multiple spellings for many words, leading to confusion and inconsistency. Vidyasagar established standardized spellings and grammatical rules, which were essential for creating uniform educational materials and literary works. This standardization was crucial for the development of a cohesive educational system and the production of textbooks and other educational resources.
4. **Phonetic Reforms:** To further simplify Bengali, Vidyasagar introduced phonetic reforms. He worked on aligning the written language more closely with its phonetic pronunciation. This alignment helped new learners to read and write more effectively, as they could rely on consistent phonetic rules. These reforms were particularly beneficial for children and non-literate adults learning to read and write for the first time.

These changes revolutionized the Bengali language, making it more accessible and functional for everyday use. Vidyasagar's efforts democratized education and literacy, enabling a broader segment of the population to participate in intellectual and cultural activities.

Writing Books for Children

One of Vidyasagar's most enduring legacies is his work in creating educational materials specifically for children. At a time when children's literature was virtually non-existent in Bengali, he recognized the critical importance of providing suitable reading materials for

> **Fun Fact**
> Vidyasagar's "Upakramanika" was unique because he included numerous examples from everyday life to explain grammatical concepts, a technique not commonly used in traditional grammar texts. This approach made learning Sanskrit grammar more intuitive and engaging for students.

young minds. Vidyasagar believed that education should start early and be grounded in clear understanding rather than rote memorization.

1. **Introduction of Children's Textbooks:** Vidyasagar wrote and published a series of textbooks designed for young learners. These books were written in simple, clear Bengali and covered fundamental subjects such as language, arithmetic, and moral lessons. Some of his most notable works in this category include:
   - *"Barnaparichay" (Introduction to the Alphabet):* This book, consisting of two parts, is perhaps Vidyasagar's most famous work. It introduced the Bengali alphabet and basic reading skills through simple exercises and engaging illustrations. "Barnaparichay" remains a staple in Bengali primary education and is still used to teach children the basics of reading and writing.
   - *"Bodhodaya" (Dawn of Knowledge):* Designed to teach basic arithmetic, "Bodhodaya" used straightforward language and practical examples to help children grasp mathematical concepts. The book covered basic operations like addition, subtraction, multiplication, and division, making mathematics less intimidating for young learners.
2. **Moral and Ethical Lessons:** Vidyasagar's children's books often included stories with moral and ethical lessons. He believed that education should not only impart academic knowledge but also instill values and good conduct. Many of his stories were drawn from Indian mythology, folklore, and his own creative imagination. They were crafted to be relatable and engaging for children, teaching them important life lessons in a manner they could understand.
3. **Educational Philosophy:** Vidyasagar's approach to education was progressive for his time. He emphasized understanding and practical knowledge over rote learning. His textbooks were designed to encourage critical thinking and comprehension. For instance, in "Barnaparichay," he included exercises that

required children to match pictures with words, helping them to connect visual cues with written language.

4. **Focus on Vernacular Education:** Vidyasagar was a strong advocate for education in the vernacular. He believed that children learned best in their mother tongue and that education should be accessible to all, regardless of their socio-economic background. His textbooks were written in simple, everyday Bengali, making them accessible to children from diverse backgrounds.

5. **Innovative Teaching Methods:** Vidyasagar introduced innovative teaching methods in his textbooks. For example, he used rhymes and songs to teach the alphabet and basic concepts. These methods were not only effective but also made learning fun for children. His emphasis on interactive and engaging learning techniques was ahead of its time and contributed to the popularity and effectiveness of his educational materials.

Vidyasagar's children's books had a profound impact on Bengali society. They played a crucial role in promoting literacy and a love for reading among children. His approach to education, which focused on understanding and critical thinking, laid the foundation for a more enlightened and educated society.

Promoting Bengali Literature

Beyond simplifying the language and writing for children, Vidyasagar was a passionate promoter of Bengali literature. He believed that a strong literary tradition was essential for cultural and intellectual growth. During the period from 1851 to 1870, he actively supported and contributed to the Bengali literary scene in various ways.

Bookseller Calcutta

1. ***Publishing and Editing:*** Vidyasagar was deeply involved in the publication and editing of numerous literary works. He understood the importance of high-quality printed materials and often provided financial and editorial support to budding writers. He was also involved in the publication of journals and magazines that featured Bengali literature, creating platforms for writers and poets to showcase their work. Some of these publications became instrumental in the literary renaissance of Bengal.

Victoria Press

2. ***Encouraging New Writers:*** Vidyasagar was a mentor to many young writers and poets. He encouraged them to write in Bengali and provided them with the necessary support to get their works published. His encouragement and guidance were instrumental in the careers of several prominent Bengali writers of the time, such as Bankim Chandra Chattopadhyay and

Michael Madhusudan Dutt. Vidyasagar's support helped these writers gain recognition and contribute to the richness of Bengali literature.

3. *Translation Work:* Recognizing the importance of exposing Bengali readers to world literature, Vidyasagar translated several classical works into Bengali. His translations were noted for their clarity and readability, making complex works accessible to a wider audience. Some of his notable translations include Shakespeare's plays and works of other European authors. These translations not only enriched Bengali literature but also provided readers with insights into different literary traditions and cultures.

Bankim Chandra Chattopadhyay

4. *Advocacy for Bengali:* Vidyasagar was a staunch advocate for the use of Bengali in education and administration. At a time when English was being promoted by the British colonial administration, he argued that education in one's mother tongue was essential for true learning and intellectual growth. His advocacy played a crucial role in the acceptance and promotion of Bengali as a medium of instruction in schools and colleges. Vidyasagar's efforts ensured that Bengali was recognized as a language of education and administration, paving the way for its continued development and use.

5. *Literary Contributions:* In addition to his work as a publisher, editor, and translator, Vidyasagar was also a prolific writer. He wrote essays, articles, and literary works that addressed various

social issues and promoted intellectual discourse. His writings were characterized by their clarity, logic, and persuasive arguments. Vidyasagar's literary contributions played a significant role in shaping public opinion and fostering a culture of critical thinking and debate in Bengali society.

Notable Works and Their Impact

Vidyasagar's literary works had a lasting impact on Bengali literature and education. Here are some of his notable works and their significance:

1. **"Barnaparichay" (Introduction to the Alphabet):** "Barnaparichay" is perhaps Vidyasagar's most famous work. Consisting of two parts, this book revolutionized primary education in Bengal. By making the alphabet and basic reading skills accessible to children, it laid the foundation for literacy and education. "Barnaparichay" is still used in Bengali schools today, a testament to its enduring relevance and effectiveness.
2. **"Bodhodaya" (Dawn of Knowledge):** This book on arithmetic simplified the teaching of mathematics for young children. Using simple language and practical examples, "Bodhodaya" helped children understand mathematical concepts. The book covered basic operations like addition, subtraction, multiplication, and division, making mathematics less intimidating and more enjoyable for children. Vidyasagar's emphasis on practical examples and clear explanations set a new standard for educational materials.
3. **"Betal Panchabinsati" (Twenty-Five Tales of Betal):** Vidyasagar's adaptation of the classic "Vikram and Betal" tales brought these engaging stories to a wider audience. The tales are known for their wit, moral lessons, and engaging storytelling. Vidyasagar's rendition made them accessible to Bengali readers and preserved their charm and educational value. The book remains popular among children and adults alike for its entertaining and thought-provoking stories.

4. ***"Shakuntala":*** Vidyasagar's translation of Kalidasa's "Abhijnanasakuntalam" into Bengali is another notable work. His translation is praised for its elegance and fidelity to the original. By translating this classical Sanskrit play, Vidyasagar made a significant contribution to Bengali literature, highlighting the richness of Indian classical literature and making it accessible to a wider audience.
5. ***"Sitar Bonobas" (Sita's Exile):*** This work is Vidyasagar's retelling of a part of the Ramayana, focusing on Sita's exile. His version is known for its emotional depth and lyrical quality. Vidyasagar's portrayal of Sita's character and her trials brought a new perspective to the epic, emphasizing the human aspects of the characters and their struggles. "Sitar Bonobas" is celebrated for its literary merit and its insightful portrayal of a key episode from the Ramayana.
6. ***Essays and Articles:*** Vidyasagar wrote numerous essays and articles addressing various social, educational, and literary issues. His writings were characterized by their logical arguments, clear language, and persuasive style. Some of his notable essays include those on widow remarriage, women's education, and social reforms. These writings had a significant impact on public opinion and played a crucial role in advancing social and educational reforms in Bengal.

The impact of Vidyasagar's work on Bengali literature and education cannot be overstated. His efforts to simplify the language, promote children's education, and support literary activities laid the foundation for a vibrant and dynamic literary tradition. Vidyasagar's notable works, such as "Barnaparichay" and "Bodhodaya," continue to be celebrated for their impact on education and literature. His legacy as a reformer, educator, and literary figure remains an inspiration to generations of Bengalis and to all those who value the power of language and education.

Ishwar Chandra Vidyasagar's contributions to language and literature during the period from 1851 to 1870 were groundbreaking and transformative. His efforts to simplify Bengali made the language

> **Fun Fact**
> Vidyasagar's translation was not just a mere linguistic conversion but also a cultural adaptation. He carefully chose words and expressions that would resonate with Bengali readers, preserving the essence of the original stories while making them more relatable.

more accessible and fostered a sense of cultural identity among Bengalis. By writing books for children, he ensured that education started early and was based on understanding rather than rote learning. His promotion of Bengali literature and support for new writers enriched the literary tradition and ensured its growth.

Vidyasagar's notable works, such as "Barnaparichay" and "Bodhodaya," continue to be celebrated for their impact on education and literature. His translations of classical works brought the richness of world literature to Bengali readers, while his essays and articles advanced social and educational reforms. Vidyasagar's legacy as a reformer, educator, and literary figure remains an inspiration to generations of Bengalis and to all those who value the power of language and education.

Through his tireless efforts, Vidyasagar not only transformed the Bengali language and literature but also laid the foundation for a more literate and enlightened society. His vision of accessible education, intellectual growth, and cultural pride continues to resonate today, making him a timeless figure in the history of Bengali literature and education.

6

Published Works of Ishwar Chandra Vidyasagar

Ishwar Chandra Vidyasagar's contributions to literature and education were monumental. His published works reflect his deep scholarship, commitment to social reform, and passion for making education accessible.

1. Betal Panchabinsati (Baital Pachisi)

One of Vidyasagar's most celebrated works is his translation of the ancient Sanskrit text "Betal Panchabinsati," also known as "Baital Pachisi" or "Twenty-five Tales of Betal." This collection of tales involves the legendary king Vikramaditya and the ghost Betal. Each story ends with a moral lesson, which Vidyasagar adeptly translated into Bengali, making it accessible to a broader audience.

2. Barnaparichay

Perhaps Vidyasagar's most influential work, "Barnaparichay" (Introduction to the Alphabet), revolutionized Bengali education. This primer for young learners systematically introduced the Bengali alphabet, making it easier for children to learn to read and write. Its simple and effective method of teaching the alphabet ensured that it became a staple in Bengali households and schools.

3. Bodhodaya

"Bodhodaya" (Awakening of Knowledge) is another significant educational text authored by Vidyasagar. It served as a reader for young students, containing simple prose and moral stories designed to instill ethical values alongside literacy skills. This book complemented "Barnaparichay" and was widely used in Bengali schools.

4. Upakramanika

"Upakramanika" (Introduction) is a textbook on Sanskrit grammar. Vidyasagar's deep understanding of Sanskrit grammar is evident in this work, which simplified complex grammatical rules for students. This book became an essential resource for students of Sanskrit and was praised for its clarity and comprehensiveness.

5. Shakuntala

Vidyasagar's adaptation of Kalidasa's classic play "Abhijnanasakuntalam" into Bengali is another notable contribution. His translation retained the poetic beauty and emotional depth of the original Sanskrit play, making it accessible to Bengali readers. This work is a testament to Vidyasagar's literary prowess and his ability to bridge classical and modern literature.

6. Rajatarangini

Vidyasagar also translated Kalhana's "Rajatarangini," a historical chronicle of the kings of Kashmir, into Bengali. This work was significant not only for its historical content but also for its linguistic and cultural importance. Vidyasagar's translation brought the rich history of Kashmir to Bengali readers, highlighting the interconnectedness of Indian culture and history.

7. Sitar Banabas

"Sitar Banabas" (Sita's Exile) is another notable work by Vidyasagar. It is a retelling of the Ramayana's episode where Sita is exiled to the forest. Vidyasagar's version is marked by its empathetic portrayal of Sita and its critique of societal norms and injustices.

8. Bangla Byakaran

"Bangla Byakaran" (Bengali Grammar) is Vidyasagar's authoritative work on Bengali grammar. This book systematically presented the rules and structure of the Bengali language, serving as a crucial resource for students and scholars. Vidyasagar's meticulous research and clear exposition made it an enduring reference in Bengali linguistics.

Legacy of Published Works

Ishwar Chandra Vidyasagar's published works have left an indelible mark on Bengali literature and education. His ability to simplify complex concepts and make them accessible to the common people was revolutionary. His works not only educated but also inspired social change, reflecting his vision of a progressive and enlightened society.

Vidyasagar's legacy continues to live on through his writings, which are still used in educational curricula and cherished by readers. His commitment to knowledge, social reform, and the empowerment of the masses makes him a towering figure in the history of Indian literature and education. His life and works remain a testament to the transformative power of education and the enduring impact of a dedicated scholar.

7

Personal Life (1820-1891)

Ishwar Chandra Vidyasagar emerged as one of the most influential figures of the 19th-century Bengal Renaissance. His life, spanning 71 years, was marked by a commitment to education, social reform, and the upliftment of society. This chapter delves into the personal aspects of his life, exploring his family, friendships, values, and his profound dedication to simple living and helping the needy.

Family and Friends

Dinamayi Devi, wife of Vidyasagar

Narayan Chandra Vidyaratna, son of Vidyasagar

Family Background: Ishwar Chandra Vidyasagar was born into a modest Brahmin family. His father, Thakurdas Bandyopadhyay, was a poor but devout man who had a significant influence on Vidyasagar's early life and values. Thakurdas was deeply committed to his son's education, even under challenging financial conditions. His mother, Bhagavati Devi, was a compassionate and resilient woman who played an equally crucial role in shaping Vidyasagar's character. She instilled in him a sense of empathy and resilience that would later define his social reforms.

Marriage and Children: Vidyasagar married Dinamayee Devi at a young age, as was customary during that period. The couple had one son, Narayan Chandra, who grew up under the guidance and principles of his illustrious father. Vidyasagar ensured that Narayan received a good education, and he later became a significant figure in the legal profession.

Relationship with Parents: Vidyasagar had a profound respect for his parents. His father, Thakurdas Bandyopadhyay, was a significant influence on his values and principles. Thakurdas instilled in him a love for learning and a strong sense of duty. Vidyasagar often mentioned his father's teachings in his writings and credited him for shaping his character. His mother, Bhagavati Devi, was a source of emotional support and inspiration. Her resilience and compassion deeply influenced Vidyasagar's outlook on life.

Friendships and Mentorship: Vidyasagar maintained close relationships with a few friends who shared his vision and supported his endeavors. Among them was Akshay Kumar Datta, a prominent writer and social reformer.

Michael Madhusudan Dutta

Their friendship was based on mutual respect and a shared commitment to the betterment of society. Another close associate was Michael Madhusudan Dutt, a renowned poet and playwright, who often sought Vidyasagar's advice and support. Vidyasagar's friendships were marked by intellectual exchanges and mutual support, with him often providing guidance and assistance to his friends.

Akshay Kumar Datta

His Values and Principles

Ishwar Chandra Vidyasagar was a man of strong values and principles, which were evident in every aspect of his life. His unwavering dedication to truth, justice, and compassion guided his actions and decisions.

1. **Commitment to Education:** Vidyasagar believed that education was the key to social reform and personal empowerment. He championed the cause of education for all, regardless of gender or caste. His establishment of numerous schools and colleges, including the Sanskrit College in Kolkata, is a testament to his belief in the transformative power of education. Vidyasagar's educational reforms were characterized by

> **Fun Fact**
> Vidyasagar's inspiration for "Barnaparichay" came from his observations of children struggling with traditional methods of learning the alphabet. He meticulously tested his methods with children before finalizing the book, ensuring its effectiveness and child-friendliness.

an emphasis on practical knowledge, scientific temper, and moral education. He introduced modern subjects alongside traditional ones, ensuring a well-rounded education for his students.

2. ***Advocacy for Women's Rights:*** Vidyasagar was a pioneering advocate for women's rights in India. He campaigned vigorously for the remarriage of widows, a practice that was taboo in the orthodox Hindu society of the time. His efforts led to the enactment of the Widow Remarriage Act of 1856. Vidyasagar also worked towards improving women's education, believing that educated women were essential for the progress of society. He established schools for girls and advocated for the inclusion of female teachers to make the environment more conducive to women's education.

3. ***Compassion and Empathy:*** Vidyasagar's actions were deeply rooted in compassion and empathy. He was known for his kindness towards the poor and the needy. His writings and reforms were aimed at alleviating the suffering of the oppressed and marginalized sections of society. Vidyasagar's empathy extended to all facets of his work, whether it was advocating for the rights of widows or ensuring that children received a quality education.

4. ***Integrity and Honesty:*** Throughout his life, Vidyasagar upheld the highest standards of integrity and honesty. He believed that moral integrity was non-negotiable and lived his life according to this principle. His financial transparency and accountability in managing educational institutions were widely respected. Vidyasagar's integrity was evident in his personal and professional dealings, earning him the trust and admiration of his peers and the public.

5. ***Rationalism and Scientific Temper:*** Vidyasagar was a rationalist who believed in questioning superstitions and irrational practices. He encouraged scientific thinking and was an ardent supporter of modern education that included science and technology. His rational approach to social issues

often put him at odds with the conservative elements of society, but he remained steadfast in his beliefs, advocating for a more enlightened and progressive society.

Simple Living

Ishwar Chandra Vidyasagar was a paragon of simplicity. Despite his prominence and the significant positions he held, he led a remarkably simple and austere life. His lifestyle was a reflection of his philosophy that one should live with minimal needs and focus on the greater good.

1. *Modest Attire:* Vidyasagar's attire was simple and traditional. He typically wore a plain dhoti and chadar (a piece of cloth draped over the shoulders). His unassuming appearance was a stark contrast to the opulence that was often associated with influential figures of his time. Vidyasagar's choice of attire was a statement of his commitment to simplicity and humility.
2. *Humble Abode:* Vidyasagar's home was modest, reflecting his disdain for unnecessary luxury. He believed in living within his means and used his resources to support his philanthropic activities rather than personal indulgence. His residence was a place of learning and simplicity, frequented by students and reformers who sought his guidance.
3. *Frugality:* Vidyasagar practiced frugality in his personal life. He was careful with his expenses and avoided any form of extravagance. This frugality allowed him to save and use his resources for charitable purposes, such as funding schools and helping the needy. Vidyasagar's financial prudence was a reflection of his belief that resources should be used for the greater good rather than personal gratification.
4. *Self-reliance:* Vidyasagar was known for his self-reliance and industriousness. He performed many tasks himself and was not dependent on others for his personal needs. His work ethic and commitment to self-reliance were exemplary. Vidyasagar's self-

reliance extended to his intellectual pursuits as well, as he often engaged in self-study and research to expand his knowledge.

Helping the Needy

Helping the needy was not just an aspect of Vidyasagar's life; it was a fundamental principle that guided his actions. His compassion for the underprivileged and marginalized was evident in his numerous philanthropic activities.

1. ***Educational Initiatives:*** Vidyasagar's most significant contribution was in the field of education. He established numerous schools and colleges, particularly for girls and the underprivileged. His efforts made education accessible to thousands who were previously denied this fundamental right. Notable among these initiatives was the establishment of the Metropolitan Institution (later known as Vidyasagar College) in 1872, which provided quality education to many students who went on to become prominent figures in various fields. Vidyasagar's educational initiatives were characterized by a focus on inclusivity and accessibility, ensuring that education was available to all sections of society.
2. ***Support for Widows and Orphans:*** Vidyasagar was deeply moved by the plight of widows and orphans. He established several institutions to support them, providing shelter, education, and vocational training. His campaign for the remarriage of widows was driven by his desire to provide them with a life of dignity and respect. Vidyasagar's efforts in this area were groundbreaking, challenging deeply entrenched social norms and advocating for the rights of marginalized women.
3. ***Medical Assistance:*** Vidyasagar also contributed to the healthcare sector by setting up medical facilities and providing financial support for the treatment of the poor. He understood that good health was essential for personal and social

development and worked towards making healthcare accessible to the needy. Vidyasagar's initiatives in healthcare were aimed at addressing the basic needs of the underprivileged, ensuring that they had access to essential medical services.

4. **Economic Support:** Vidyasagar provided financial assistance to those in need, including scholarships for students, stipends for widows, and support for struggling families. His financial aid was often extended anonymously, reflecting his genuine desire to help without seeking recognition. Vidyasagar's economic support initiatives were characterized by a focus on sustainability and empowerment, helping individuals and families to become self-reliant.

5. **Legal Reforms:** Vidyasagar's advocacy extended to legal reforms aimed at protecting the rights of the disadvantaged. His efforts in securing the Widow Remarriage Act and opposing child marriage were driven by his commitment to social justice and equality. Vidyasagar's legal reforms were instrumental in bringing about significant changes in the social fabric of Bengal, promoting gender equality and social justice.

6. **Personal Acts of Kindness:** Vidyasagar's kindness was not limited to his public life; he was known for his personal acts of generosity. Stories of him helping individuals in distress, providing shelter to the homeless, and feeding the hungry are numerous. He often went out of his way to help those in need, demonstrating his deep empathy and compassion. Vidyasagar's personal acts of kindness were a reflection of his belief in the inherent dignity and worth of every individual.

Relationship with Family and Friends

Vidyasagar's relationships with his family and friends were characterized by love, respect, and mutual support. Despite his busy schedule and numerous responsibilities, he remained a devoted family man and a loyal friend.

1. **Relationship with Parents:** Vidyasagar had a profound respect for his parents. His father, Thakurdas Bandyopadhyay, was a significant influence on his values and principles. Thakurdas instilled in him a love for learning and a strong sense of duty. Vidyasagar often mentioned his father's teachings in his writings and credited him for shaping his character. His mother, Bhagavati Devi, was a source of emotional support and inspiration. Her resilience and compassion deeply influenced Vidyasagar's outlook on life.
2. **Marriage and Children:** Vidyasagar's marriage to Dinamayee Devi was arranged, as was customary at the time. Despite the constraints of an arranged marriage, Vidyasagar maintained a respectful and caring relationship with his wife. They had one son, Narayan Chandra, who became a prominent legal professional. Vidyasagar ensured that Narayan received a good education and was well-prepared for his future.
3. **Friendships:** Vidyasagar's friendships were based on mutual respect and shared ideals. His friendship with Akshay Kumar Datta, a fellow reformer and intellectual, was particularly significant. They collaborated on several educational and social initiatives, and their partnership was instrumental in advancing the cause of social reform in Bengal. Michael Madhusudan Dutt, a renowned poet and playwright, also shared a close bond with Vidyasagar. Their friendship was marked by intellectual exchanges and mutual support, with Vidyasagar often providing guidance and assistance to Dutt.
4. **Mentorship:** Vidyasagar was a mentor to many young writers, educators, and social reformers. He encouraged them to pursue their goals with dedication and integrity. His guidance and support helped many of his protégés achieve success and make significant contributions to society. Vidyasagar's mentorship extended beyond professional advice; he often provided financial and emotional support to those in need.

Ishwar Chandra Vidyasagar's personal life was a reflection of his deep-rooted values, principles, and unwavering commitment to simplicity and service. His relationships with family and friends were characterized by love, respect, and mutual support. His contributions to education, social reform, and the upliftment of society had a lasting impact, laying the foundation for a more enlightened and just society. Vidyasagar's legacy as a reformer, educator, and philanthropist continues to inspire and guide future generations, reminding us of the enduring power of compassion, integrity, and dedication to the greater good.

Through his tireless efforts, Vidyasagar not only transformed the Bengali language and literature but also laid the foundation for a more literate and enlightened society. His vision of accessible education, intellectual growth, and cultural pride continues to resonate today, making him a timeless figure in the history of Bengali literature and education. His life serves as a testament to the power of education, the importance of social justice, and the impact of a life dedicated to the service of others.

8

Legacy (1891-Present)

Ishwar Chandra Vidyasagar's legacy is marked by a plethora of honors and achievements that recognize his profound contributions to education, literature, and social reform in India. His impact continues to resonate across generations, influencing cultural identity, educational policies, and social justice movements.

Contributions to Indian Society

1. *Educational Reforms and Institutions:* Ishwar Chandra Vidyasagar's dedication to education led to the establishment of several institutions that transformed the educational landscape of Bengal. His founding of the Metropolitan Institution (Vidyasagar College) in Kolkata exemplified his vision of providing modern education accessible to all, regardless of caste or gender. This institution became a model for subsequent educational reforms in India, emphasizing a curriculum that blended traditional values with contemporary knowledge.

2. *Literary and Linguistic Contributions:* Vidyasagar's impact on Bengali literature

> **Fun Fact**
> Vidyasagar's "Bangla Byakaran" was one of the first comprehensive grammar books for Bengali, and it set the standard for subsequent works in the field. His approach to grammar was innovative, as he incorporated examples from contemporary Bengali literature and everyday speech to illustrate grammatical rules.

and language was profound. His simplification of Bengali grammar and his creation of textbooks that catered to the needs of students from diverse backgrounds helped popularize Bengali as a language of instruction and intellectual discourse. His literary works, including essays, poems, and translations, are celebrated for their clarity, simplicity, and social relevance, making him a towering figure in Bengali literary history.

Influence on Future Generations

1. *Educational Philosophy and Policy:* Vidyasagar's educational philosophy emphasized the importance of practical knowledge, moral development, and social responsibility. His advocacy for inclusive education laid the groundwork for policies aimed at universalizing primary education and promoting higher education among marginalized communities. Institutions like Vidyasagar University in Midnapore, West Bengal, continue to uphold his ideals of academic excellence and social equity.
2. *Cultural and Social Impact:* Vidyasagar's role in the Bengal Renaissance, a cultural and intellectual revival in Bengal, promoted rational thinking, scientific inquiry, and social reform. His efforts to modernize Bengali literature and promote women's education challenged orthodoxies and contributed to a broader cultural awakening that reshaped Bengal's identity and ethos.

Honors and Achievements of Ishwar Chandra Vidyasagar

1. Honorary Titles and Recognition:
- "Vidyasagar": Ishwar Chandra Vidyasagar was bestowed with the honorary title "Vidyasagar," meaning "Ocean of Knowledge," in recognition of his profound erudition and scholarly contributions, particularly in the fields of education, literature, and social reform. This title

underscored his status as a preeminent intellectual figure of his time and acknowledged his significant impact on Bengali culture and society.

1970 Stamp of India

125 Years of Vidyasagar University, 1998

2. Commemorative Stamps and Coins:
- Postage Stamps: The Government of India has issued commemorative postage stamps featuring Ishwar Chandra Vidyasagar's likeness to honor his contributions to education and literature. These stamps serve as a tribute to his enduring legacy and recognize his pivotal role in promoting literacy, social reform, and cultural enlightenment in India.

3. Educational Institutions Named After Him:
- Vidyasagar University: Established in 1981 in Midnapore, West Bengal, Vidyasagar University stands as a testament to Ishwar Chandra Vidyasagar's lasting influence on higher education in India. The university was named in his honor to commemorate his visionary efforts in advancing education, fostering intellectual growth, and promoting social equity through accessible and inclusive educational opportunities.

4. Literary Works and Contributions:
- Literary Accolades: Ishwar Chandra Vidyasagar's literary contributions, including his acclaimed textbooks and

literary compositions, have earned him widespread recognition for their educational value, linguistic clarity, and cultural significance. His meticulous simplification of Bengali grammar and his role in standardizing the language for modern usage have solidified his legacy as a seminal figure in Bengali literature and language reform.

5. Social Reform Efforts:
- *Advocac*y for Widow Remarriage: One of Vidyasagar's most enduring achievements was his pivotal role in advocating for the Widow Remarriage Act of 1856. This landmark legislation, which he fervently championed, aimed to abolish the social stigma and legal barriers associated with widowhood in India, thereby empowering widows to reclaim their rights to marital happiness and social acceptance. The enactment of this progressive law remains a testament to Vidyasagar's unwavering commitment to gender equality and social justice.

6. Statues and Memorials:
- *Public C*ommemoration: Ishwar Chandra Vidyasagar is honored with numerous statues and memorials erected across India, particularly in West Bengal, to commemorate his exemplary life and enduring contributions to Indian society. These statues serve as poignant reminders of his remarkable legacy as a scholar, educator, reformer, and philanthropist, inspiring generations with his ideals of knowledge, compassion, and social responsibility.

7. Government Recognitions:
- *National H*onors: Posthumously, Ishwar Chandra Vidyasagar has been honored by the Government of India with national awards and accolades in recognition of his exceptional contributions to education, literature, and social reform. These prestigious honors highlight his profound impact on shaping the intellectual, cultural, and social fabric of modern India, cementing his status as a revered figure in the annals of Indian history.

8. Philanthropic Contributions:
- *Hu*manitarian Endeavors: Vidyasagar's philanthropic initiatives, marked by his personal commitment and selfless dedication to uplift the underprivileged and marginalized communities, have earned him admiration and respect for his exemplary humanitarianism. His enduring legacy of compassionate service continues to inspire philanthropic endeavors aimed at promoting social welfare, empowering disadvantaged groups, and fostering inclusive development across India.

Ishwar Chandra Vidyasagar's honors and achievements illuminate his stature as a visionary scholar, educator, reformer, and philanthropist whose impact on Indian society remains profound and enduring. His recognition through awards, institutions, and commemorative honors underscores his pivotal role in shaping modern India's intellectual, cultural, and social fabric. Vidyasagar's life and legacy continue to inspire generations with his dedication to knowledge, social justice, and the advancement of human welfare, embodying the ideals of enlightenment and progressivism that define his enduring legacy.

His legacy as a scholar, educator, reformer, and philanthropist continues to resonate in the hearts and minds of people across India and beyond. His contributions to education, literature, and social reform have left an indelible mark on Indian society, inspiring generations to uphold the values of justice, equality, and compassion. As a visionary leader of the Bengal Renaissance, Vidyasagar's life serves as a guiding light for those committed to the pursuit of knowledge, social progress, and human dignity.

9

His Interests

Early Life in Birsingha: Ishwar Chandra Vidyasagar was born on September 26, 1820, in the village of Birsingha, located in the Midnapore district of Bengal (present-day West Bengal, India). His birthplace, a rural setting surrounded by natural beauty and simplicity, deeply influenced his outlook on life and his later commitment to rural education and social welfare. Growing up in Birsingha, Vidyasagar experienced the traditional Bengali way of life, characterized by close-knit communities and agricultural practices.

Astronomical Curiosity: From a young age, Vidyasagar exhibited a keen interest in astronomy. He would often spend hours observing the night sky, studying constellations, and marveling at celestial phenomena. This early fascination with astronomy not only sparked his scientific curiosity but also instilled in him a profound appreciation for the wonders of the universe.

Botanical Enthusiasm: Apart from astronomy, Vidyasagar harbored a deep love for botany. He cultivated a garden at his home in Calcutta (now Kolkata), where he meticulously tended to a variety of plants and flowers. His botanical pursuits provided him with both relaxation and intellectual stimulation, offering a peaceful retreat from his rigorous academic and social reform activities.

Contributions to Bengali Printing: Vidyasagar made significant contributions to advancing Bengali printing technology during the 19th century. Recognizing the importance of printed literature in spreading knowledge and fostering intellectual growth, he collaborated closely with printers to improve typesetting techniques and printing quality. His efforts played a crucial role in making books more accessible and affordable to the general public, thereby promoting literacy and education across Bengal.

Calligraphic Excellence: Known for his exquisite handwriting and calligraphy skills, Vidyasagar's manuscripts and letters were highly esteemed for their clarity, elegance, and precision. His meticulous attention to detail in calligraphy reflected his reverence for the written word and underscored his commitment to maintaining high standards of literary expression.

Recognition by British Authorities: Despite his advocacy for Indian languages and cultural traditions, Vidyasagar earned the respect and admiration of British colonial officials for his intellectual prowess and integrity. In 1851, he was appointed as the principal of Sanskrit College in Calcutta (now Kolkata), a prestigious institution of higher learning. This appointment underscored his academic credentials and administrative acumen, highlighting his pivotal role in shaping Sanskrit education in colonial Bengal.

Advocacy for Indigenous Medicine: Vidyasagar was a vocal proponent of indigenous Indian medical systems, including Ayurveda and Unani medicine. He believed in integrating traditional healing practices with modern medical knowledge to enhance healthcare accessibility and efficacy for the masses. His advocacy for indigenous medicine reflected his holistic approach to public health and well-being, emphasizing the importance of culturally rooted healthcare solutions.

Love for Classical Music: Beyond his scholarly pursuits, Vidyasagar had a profound appreciation for classical Indian music, particularly Hindustani

> **Fun Fact**
>
> Vidyasagar's translation of "Shakuntala" was initially met with skepticism by some purists who believed that the beauty of Kalidasa's poetry could not be captured in Bengali. However, Vidyasagar's skillful translation won widespread acclaim and silenced his critics.

and Carnatic genres. He actively attended music concerts and supported musicians who dedicated themselves to preserving and propagating traditional musical forms. His patronage of classical music underscored his broader cultural interests and commitment to promoting artistic heritage in Bengal.

Friendship with Michael Madhusudan Dutt: Vidyasagar maintained a close friendship with Michael Madhusudan Dutt, the eminent Bengali poet and playwright known for his literary innovations and social critiques. Their intellectual camaraderie enriched Bengal's literary and cultural landscape, fostering a vibrant exchange of ideas and perspectives. Both Vidyasagar and Dutt shared a deep commitment to literary excellence and societal reform, contributing to the dynamic intellectual milieu of 19th-century Bengal.

Advocacy for Animal Welfare: Vidyasagar was an outspoken advocate for animal welfare and ethical treatment of animals. He expressed concern for the well-being of animals and supported initiatives aimed at preventing cruelty and promoting compassionate treatment. His advocacy for animal rights reflected his broader humanitarian principles and commitment to fostering empathy and respect for all living beings.

Commitment to Environmental Conservation: Concerned about environmental degradation and its impact on human health, Vidyasagar advocated for sustainable agricultural practices and conservation of natural resources. He emphasized the importance of ecological balance and responsible stewardship of the environment to ensure the well-being of present and future generations. His holistic approach to environmental conservation resonated with his broader vision of societal progress and human flourishing.

Enduring Popularity and Commemoration: Ishwar Chandra Vidyasagar's legacy continues to be celebrated and revered in India and beyond. Numerous educational institutions, streets, and cultural organizations bear his name as a tribute to his enduring contributions to education, social reform, and literature. His statues and memorials serve as reminders of his profound impact on Indian society and inspire generations to uphold his ideals of knowledge, compassion, and social justice.

Stories from His Life

Raja Ram Mohan Roy

Meeting Raja Ram Mohan Roy
One of the defining moments in Ishwar Chandra Vidyasagar's life occurred in 1839 during his formative years as a student at the Sanskrit College in Calcutta. It was here that he had the privilege of attending a transformative lecture delivered by none other than

Raja Ram Mohan Roy, the eminent social reformer and founder of the Brahmo Samaj. Roy, a visionary ahead of his time, captivated the young Vidyasagar with his impassioned advocacy for social reform, rationalism, and the urgent need to eradicate regressive social practices that plagued Indian society.

At the time of this encounter, Vidyasagar was already recognized for his exceptional intellect and insatiable thirst for knowledge. Roy's lecture, however, proved to be more than just a scholarly discourse; it ignited a fervent passion within Vidyasagar to actively challenge entrenched societal injustices and advocate for progressive reforms. Roy, impressed by Vidyasagar's intellectual prowess and earnest commitment to social change, took him under his wing, recognizing in him a future leader and torchbearer for enlightened reform in India.

Under Roy's mentorship, Vidyasagar delved deeper into the principles of enlightenment, rational thought, and humanistic values. Roy's emphasis on individual liberty, social equality, and the emancipation of women left an indelible mark on Vidyasagar's evolving worldview and moral compass. This formative mentorship laid the foundation for Vidyasagar's lifelong dedication to challenging oppressive customs and advocating for social justice, setting him on a path of intellectual inquiry and humanitarian action that would define his legacy.

Friendship with Debendranath Tagore

Ishwar Chandra Vidyasagar cultivated a profound and enduring friendship with Debendranath Tagore, a prominent figure in the Brahmo Samaj movement and the father of Rabindranath Tagore, India's first Nobel laureate in literature. Their friendship blossomed from a shared commitment to intellectual inquiry, social reform, and cultural renewal in 19th-century Bengal.

Debendranath Tagore, renowned for his visionary thinking and dedication to religious and social reform, held Vidyasagar in high regard for his scholarly achievements and unwavering

Debendranath Tagore

advocacy for education. The two intellectuals collaborated closely on various initiatives aimed at advancing educational reforms, promoting women's rights, and fostering social welfare within the Brahmo Samaj and broader society.

Together, Vidyasagar and Debendranath Tagore played instrumental roles in strengthening the Brahmo Samaj's efforts to challenge orthodox Hindu practices and promote a more inclusive and progressive societal ethos. Their partnership not only enriched intellectual discourse but also catalyzed practical initiatives aimed at uplifting marginalized communities and empowering individuals through education and social reform.

Intellectual Rivalry with Bankim Chandra Chattopadhyay

In addition to his collaborations and friendships, Ishwar Chandra Vidyasagar engaged in spirited intellectual exchanges and occasional rivalries with contemporaries like Bankim Chandra Chattopadhyay. Chattopadhyay, a towering figure in Bengali literature and a passionate nationalist, represented a contrasting intellectual force in 19th-century Bengal, known for his literary innovations and fervent advocacy of Indian nationalism. Vidyasagar's intellectual pursuits centered on promoting social reform, education, and humanitarianism as essential pillars of societal progress. His emphasis on eradicating social evils such as child marriage, caste discrimination, and the mistreatment of widows often clashed with Chattopadhyay's nationalist fervor and cultural revivalism. Their intellectual rivalry, marked by debates and dialogues in literary circles, underscored the diversity of thought and ideological tensions that characterized Bengal's intellectual landscape during this transformative period.

Despite their ideological differences, Vidyasagar and Chattopadhyay's interactions contributed to the vibrant intellectual milieu of 19th-century Bengal, stimulating critical discourse on pressing social issues and cultural revival. While Vidyasagar focused on advocating for progressive social reforms and leveraging education for societal transformation, Chattopadhyay articulated nationalist sentiments and urged cultural resurgence as a means to assert Indian identity against colonial domination.

Ishwar Chandra Vidyasagar's relationships with Raja Ram Mohan Roy, Debendranath Tagore, and Bankim Chandra Chattopadhyay exemplify his multifaceted engagement with Bengal's intellectual and cultural renaissance during the 19th century. These interactions not only shaped Vidyasagar's intellectual development but also influenced broader societal movements towards social reform, cultural revival, and national awakening in colonial India. Vidyasagar's journey from a young scholar with a prodigious memory to a fearless advocate for social justice underscores the importance of intellectual curiosity, moral integrity, and a steadfast commitment to principles of equality and human dignity. His legacy serves as a beacon of hope and inspiration, reminding us of the enduring impact of individual action and collective effort in advancing social progress.

Bankim Chandra Chattopadhyay

In celebrating Ishwar Chandra Vidyasagar's legacy, we honor not only his intellectual brilliance and moral clarity but also his unwavering dedication to the betterment of society. His life story challenges us to confront injustice, champion the rights of the marginalized, and strive for a world where compassion, justice, and equality prevail.

Stories from His Life

Ishwar Chandra Vidyasagar's life was filled with remarkable stories that highlight his intelligence, compassion, and dedication to social reform. This commitment laid the foundation for Vidyasagar's lifelong love for learning and reform.

The Name "Vidyasagar"

One of the most famous stories from Vidyasagar's early life is about how he earned the title "Vidyasagar," which means "Ocean of Knowledge." As a young boy, Vidyasagar showed extraordinary brilliance in his studies. His knowledge of Sanskrit, literature, and philosophy was so profound that his teachers were amazed. At the age of 21, after a rigorous examination at the Sanskrit College in Calcutta, he was awarded the title "Vidyasagar" by the scholars and pundits of the college. This title was a testament to his exceptional intellectual abilities and became a permanent part of his identity.

Struggles and Perseverance

Another poignant story from his life is about the struggles he faced during his early education. Vidyasagar had to walk miles to reach Calcutta for his studies. He often studied under street lamps because his family could not afford enough oil for a lamp at home. Despite these hardships, his determination never wavered. He excelled in his studies and became a respected scholar, showcasing the strength of his character and his unwavering commitment to education.

Helping a Poor Widow

Vidyasagar's compassion and empathy were evident in his numerous acts of kindness. One such story is about how he helped a poor widow. While he was the principal of Sanskrit College, he encountered a destitute widow begging for help. Touched by her plight, Vidyasagar not only provided her with financial assistance but also helped her secure a job. This act of kindness was just one of many, reflecting his deep sense of social responsibility and his commitment to improving the lives of the less fortunate.

Reforming Education

As an educationist, Vidyasagar made significant reforms that transformed the educational landscape of Bengal. He introduced the study of Western science and literature alongside traditional Sanskrit education. He believed that a modern education system should encompass a broad spectrum of knowledge, including humanities and sciences. His reforms laid the foundation for the modern education system in Bengal and provided students with a more comprehensive and holistic education.

Campaign for Widow Remarriage

One of the most impactful stories from Vidyasagar's life is his relentless campaign for widow remarriage. In 19th century Bengal, widows were subjected to severe social stigma and isolation. Vidyasagar was deeply moved by their suffering and took up the cause of advocating for their right to remarry. He faced immense opposition from conservative sections of society and even from his peers. Despite this, he succeeded in convincing the British government to pass the Widow Remarriage Act of 1856. This was a landmark achievement that paved the way for social reform and improved the lives of countless widows.

Inspirational Incidents

Vidyasagar's life is replete with inspirational incidents that underscore his courage, integrity, and progressive thinking.

Confronting the Orthodoxy

One such incident involves his bold confrontation with orthodox Brahmins who opposed his reformist ideas. Vidyasagar, despite being a Brahmin himself, was fearless in challenging the rigid and regressive customs of his community. He argued that true religion and morality lay in compassion and justice, not in blind adherence to outdated practices. His fearless stand against orthodoxy inspired many young reformers and established him as a leading figure in the social reform movement.

Establishing Schools for Girls

Vidyasagar's commitment to women's education is another source of inspiration. He believed that education was the key to women's empowerment and worked tirelessly to establish schools for girls. Despite facing societal resistance and financial constraints, he succeeded in setting up several girls' schools across Bengal. His efforts laid the groundwork for the future progress of women's education in India.

Rescuing a Sinking Boat

A particularly heroic incident from Vidyasagar's life occurred when he was on a boat journey. The boat he was traveling in began to sink due to a sudden storm. While others panicked, Vidyasagar remained calm and helped rescue the passengers. His composure and bravery in the face of danger were widely praised and added to his reputation as a man of strong character.

Conclusion

Ishwar Chandra Vidyasagar's life was a testament to the power of education, compassion, and social reform. Born into humble beginnings, he rose to become a towering figure in 19th-century Bengal, leaving an indelible mark on Indian society. His contributions to education, particularly his efforts to modernize the curriculum and promote women's education, laid the foundation for future generations. Vidyasagar's campaign for widow remarriage was a pioneering step towards social justice, showcasing his courage in confronting deep-seated societal norms.

Vidyasagar at the end of his life

Vidyasagar's intellectual prowess earned him the title "Ocean of Knowledge," but it was his humanity and unwavering dedication to improving the lives of others that truly defined his legacy. His life's stories, from helping destitute widows to establishing schools for girls, reflect a man deeply committed to the principles of equality and justice. His bold confrontations with orthodoxy and his perseverance in the face of adversity inspire us to challenge the status quo and strive for a more inclusive and compassionate society.

From the streets of Calcutta, where he studied under street lamps, to the halls of the Sanskrit College, where he introduced groundbreaking educational reforms, Vidyasagar's journey was one of relentless pursuit of knowledge and unwavering commitment to social change. His legacy continues to inspire educators, reformers, and activists around the world.

In remembering Vidyasagar, we not only honor his contributions but also draw valuable lessons from his life. His story teaches us the importance of perseverance, the value of education, and the necessity of compassion in creating a just society. By following his example, we can work towards a future where education is accessible to all, social justice prevails, and the marginalized are uplifted.

Ishwar Chandra Vidyasagar's life is a beacon of hope and a source of inspiration, reminding us that one person's determination and empathy can bring about profound and lasting change. His legacy is a testament to the enduring power of knowledge, kindness, and reform, guiding us towards a better and more equitable world.

Timeline of Ishwar Chandra Vidyasagar's Life

Early Life and Education

1820 - Birth:
- **September 26, 1820:** Ishwar Chandra Bandopadhyay is born in the village of Birsingha, Bengal Presidency (now West Bengal, India).

1829 - Move to Calcutta:
- Ishwar Chandra moves to Calcutta with his father, Thakurdas Bandyopadhyay, to pursue better educational opportunities.

1829 - Admission to Sanskrit College:
- Admitted to Sanskrit College in Calcutta, beginning his formal education in Sanskrit literature, grammar, and philosophy.

Academic Achievements

1839 - Title of Vidyasagar:
- Earns the title "Vidyasagar" (Ocean of Knowledge) for his mastery of Sanskrit grammar and literature, especially the "Siddhanta Kaumudi."

1841 - Graduation:
- Graduates from Sanskrit College with the highest honors, marking the completion of his formal education.

1841 - Appointment at Fort William College:
- Appointed as head pandit at Fort William College, responsible for teaching and translating texts.

Professional and Reformist Milestones

1850 - Role at Sanskrit College:
- Returns to Sanskrit College as Assistant Secretary. Later becomes Principal and implements significant educational reforms.

1851 - Principal of Sanskrit College:
- Appointed as the principal of Sanskrit College, where he modernizes the curriculum and improves educational standards.

1854 - Female Education Movement:
- Plays a crucial role in establishing the first school for girls in Calcutta, advocating for female education and challenging societal norms.

1855 - Publication of Barnaparichay:
- Publishes "Barnaparichay" (Introduction to the Alphabet), a primer that revolutionizes Bengali education and becomes a staple in schools.

1856 - Widow Remarriage Act:
- Instrumental in the passage of the Hindu Widows' Remarriage Act, which legalizes the remarriage of Hindu widows.

1865 - Establishment of Metropolitan Institution:
- Founds the Metropolitan Institution (later known as Vidyasagar College) in Calcutta to provide higher education in both English and Bengali.

Later Years

1872 - Retirement:
- Retires from public life and moves to his ancestral village, continuing to work on his literary projects and educational initiatives.

1891 - Death:
- *July 29, 1891:* Ishwar Chandra Vidyasagar passes away in Calcutta, leaving behind a legacy of educational and social reform.

Excerpts from Vidyasagar's Works

Ishwar Chandra Vidyasagar wrote several influential books that contributed significantly to Bengali literature, education, and social reform. Here are some interesting excerpts from his works:

"Borno Porichoy" (Introduction to Letters)

Excerpt: This book is a primer on Bengali alphabets and is still used to teach young children how to read and write Bengali. It begins with:

"অ - আম" (A - Aam, meaning Mango)
"আ - আকাশ" (Aa - Aakash, meaning Sky)

This simple yet profound approach helped children learn the basics of their language through familiar words.

"Betal Panchabinsati" (The Twenty-five Tales of Betal)

Excerpt: This book is a Bengali adaptation of the ancient Sanskrit collection of tales, "Vikram and Betal." Vidyasagar's adaptation made these stories accessible to the common people of Bengal.

"মহারাজ বিক্রমাদিত্য ছিলেন এক প্রজাবৎসল, বীর ও ন্যায়পরায়ণ রাজা। একদিন তিনি বেতাল নামক এক ভূতের সংস্পর্শে আসেন, যে তাকে নানা রকমের ধাঁধা জিজ্ঞেস করত।"

Translation: King Vikramaditya was a benevolent, brave, and just ruler. One day, he came into contact with a ghost named Betal, who asked him various riddles.

"Sitar Bonobas" (Sita's Exile)

Excerpt: This book narrates the story of Sita's exile from the epic Ramayana, focusing on her struggles and resilience.

"সীতা বললেন, 'আমার ধর্ম পালনই আমার জীবনের মূল লক্ষ্য। আমি সমস্ত প্রতিকূলতা সহ্য করব, তবুও আমার কর্তব্য থেকে সরে আসব না।'"

Translation: Sita said, 'Adhering to my duty is the primary goal of my life. I will endure all adversities, but I will not deviate from my duty.'

"Barnaparichay" (Parts 1 and 2)

Excerpt: Another important primer, "Barnaparichay," was designed to teach Bengali children the fundamentals of the language.

"আসুন আমরা অক্ষর চিনে নেই। অ থেকে আ, ক থেকে চন্দ্রবিন্দু। সব অক্ষর মিলে গঠিত হয় আমাদের ভাষা।"

Translation: Let us recognize the letters. From 'A' to 'Aa,' from 'Ka' to 'Chandrabindu.' All letters together form our language.

"Shakuntala"

Excerpt: This is Vidyasagar's Bengali adaptation of Kalidasa's famous Sanskrit play "Abhijnanasakuntalam."

"দুষ্মন্ত বললেন, 'সৌন্দর্য্য যে অমরত্বের একটি অংশ, তোমার মধ্যে তার পরিপূর্ণ প্রকাশ ঘটেছে। তোমার রূপে আমি মুগ্ধ।'"

Translation: Dushyanta said, 'Beauty is a part of immortality, and in you, it is fully manifested. I am enchanted by your beauty.'

"Betal Panchabinsati"

Excerpt: This collection of stories involves clever plots and moral lessons, often presented through riddles and answers.

"বেতাল বললেন, 'যদি তোমার বিচার সঠিক হয়, তবে তুমি মর্ত্যে ফিরে যাবে; আর যদি না হয়, তবে আমি তোমাকে তোমার পুণ্যফলের অধিকারী করব।'"

Translation: Betal said, 'If your judgment is correct, you will return to the mortal world; if not, I will make you entitled to the fruits of your virtue.'

These excerpts provide a glimpse into Vidyasagar's literary style and his efforts to make complex subjects accessible to the general populace. His works remain highly regarded in Bengali literature and education.